TO COMPARE

XUELA ZHANG

Fonograf Editions
Edited by Jeff Alessandrelli, Ellena Basada & Adie B. Steckel
Portland, OR & New York City, NY

Copyright © 2026 • Xuela Zhang • All rights reserved
Cover and text design by Mike Corrao

First Edition, First Printing
FONO44

Published by Fonograf Editions
www.fonografeditions.com

For information about permission to reuse any material from this book, please contact Fonograf Ed. at info@fonografeditions.com.

Distributed by NYU Press
NYUPress.org

The manufacturer's authorized representative in the EU for product safety is Mare Nostrum Group B.V., Mauritskade 21D, 1091 GC Amsterdam, The Netherlands.
Email: gpsr@mare-nostrum.co.uk.

[clmp]

Fonograf Editions is a proud member of the Community of Literary Magazines and Presses

ISBN: 978-1-964499-46-8
ISBN (ebook): 978-1-964499-58-1
LCCN: 2025942576

TO COMPARE

FONOGRAF EDITIONS

CONTENT

3 | Quarantine
7 | To Compare
23 | Prelude to Translator's Note
31 | Journey to the West
45 | Translator's Note
66 | To Compare
70 | Land Art

73 | Notes
75 | Acknowledgments

有始也者，有未始有始也者，有未始有夫未始有始也者。有有也者，有无也者，有未始有无也者，有未始有夫未始有无也者。俄而有无矣，而未知有无之果孰有孰无也。今我则已有谓矣，而未知吾所谓之其果有谓乎，其果无谓乎？

There is beginning. There is a time before beginning. There is a time before the time before beginning. There is being. There is nonbeing. There is a stage before nonbeing. There is a stage before the stage before nonbeing. Suddenly there is being and nonbeing. Still, as for being and nonbeing, I do not know which is really being and which is nonbeing. Now I have just said something, but I do not know whether what I have said is really saying something or not.

—"On the Equality of Things," *Zhuangzi / Chuang Tzu*, trans. Victor H. Mair

Quarantine

In this real, rolling, crisis
of justifiable abstractions,

loneliness overlapped
without violence.

The daylight,
as usual, faithful.

Occasionally a wind
refines a way of self-

possession. On our walks,
the air, separating the trees,

and the animals,
separating the grass

with the rush
of small entireties,

say *listen,*
you need not have noticed.

I think about the things
I need not have noticed—

the tidal over- and under-
estimations.

Quarantine

The sea had a way of turning.
It made recoiling
a slow and constant sensation.

The entire shore breathed
regardless of tension,
an endless version of the pelvis.

She said you could not see
this muscle, but it would move.
Imagine this part of you

sucking up a piece of tissue.
Very counter-intuitive, she added.
You caught yourself breathing

carefully, but wrongly.
He insisted on talking; you looked
up, and became absorbed

in the pink, rubbed clouds.
Elsewhere, it was experienced
as "the tornado." *Was it unbelievable*

to see one house destroyed,
and the one next to it
untouched, asked the anchor.

Yeah, unbelievable.

To Compare

To Compare

The lights sliding up
and the lights sliding down

are simply the features
of a curvy city.

Framed, all curves hang.
This land serves solely

the momentum of light.
From underneath

the fabric roof,
the shuttle takes us

into a smaller city.
The lights receding,

the lurking interior
becomes precise.

The more you learn,
the more you rely on

abstruse information.
In the analysis,

the elements are
treated as separable

like sound and meaning
in translation.

Your decision
is not about words,

but the exoticized
range of choices.

Has language
passed you by

like a curvy city
or shielded

and isolated you,
an illuminated vehicle

against the flooding
tenors of light?

To Compare

I encounter the self
that briefly stopped moving.

How to recover,
among letters, the craft?

This arrangement
of characters:

compounded,
counterpointed.

Things overflow
as I peel off the skin

which was also
holding the form.

Transition from
a language of extant

dreams to a dream
of extant language.

Translating like
holding the fluid

that used to be the limbs
of ice sculptures.

The "sages,"
their legs disappear

and they move
reluctant as mermaids,

as in "Prufrock."
The slow movement

of their lips
looks like singing.

What was the price
a language had

to pay—to make me
relatable?

I guess, from now on,
I give you no tropes.

So many images
used to carry

the language's own
irony, not yours.

But some say
translation is love.

Maybe, like love,
it has to be secured

in vast insecurity.
In Pound's first

translation of Chinese
(when he did not know

Chinese), he missed much
in the initial poem.

Later, he retranslated.
His emphasis changed

from
    "Horses, his horses even, are tired. They were strong."
to
  "(no one feels half of what we know)."

To Compare

The unexpected
intervals in his tone

converged into
another type of image,

a switch from the voice
of someone into

the lower, clearer voice
of someone's translator.

In college, Saskia,
in her poetry

workshop, said
a group of psychologists

had asked people to spit
into a cup of water,

and drink. Nobody would.
But it came out of

your own body, she said.
We still wouldn't

without switching tongue
and after, utter everything

as only understanding—
the white, burdened air

of someone hard-working
for another way to feel.

To Compare

Some days we look just like how we are perceived: foreigners, fussing. In the classroom of English: the low podium of commas, the plastic seats of pronouns. Have you seen Eurovision, where most nations sing in English? Afterwards we'd wonder: how much Kafka is in my Kafka? (The translation we have, we are happy with it, here on campus, though imagine you were Kafka. Perhaps he'd decide to be happy—by then happiness would have become a decision, more than a feeling.) We feel at home being stuck in (not out of) translation. A desire to mean might be a desire to feel—on and off what touched.

To Compare

At some point, the playground
resembled a landscape

in unnatural undulation.
May we distinguish

the clarity of this land
from its retreat?

I played playlists, immersed
in bath water.

I considered the meaning
of disappointments

in transnational life.
We might have to relearn

how to stimulate each other.
The world, being small,

competed with all
our untranslatables.

It disappointed us quicker
than we had, individually.

I stayed, as how I had
stayed in language.

To Compare

There is a salmon-colored path in the middle; the trees on both sides narrow smoothly like two digital walls. But things could not have been digital. Still, the trees bow in the same softened manner like roasted asparagus. An image gets into the stomach. You want to look into the body like looking into a washing machine. Be aware of the desire to render the body transparent: the non-diabetic influencer carries a glucose monitor in order to feel safe. In a study on the modernist, you use the phrase "early globalization." When would we catch up with our connection? May the world, like a loose ball of wearables, roll behind a sheet of glass instead of this wall of warm skin.

The network turned its translations of the world into a business model…

Watching it all, I felt the familiar fog that descends when something is lost in translation, when someone talks about something you share—in this case, a country—using details that are unrecognizable.

—Megan Garber

Prelude to Translator's Note

Instead of figuring out the conditions of trust,
I decided to trust my own condition.
Things quieted down.

There was a nice view over this bridge.
I recognized, simultaneously, generosities
and waywardness.

The way the water
flowed, somewhat insistent,
at times like an understanding,

at times like an attitude.
Then I turned back slowly
like the large pet of truth.

Whatever language had been used,
I hoped we had been courageous enough
to know what we had not known

regarding our ignorance.
There was the obliquity
of the planet in the way

you briefly looked
into me.
Your eyes waited.

✳

I came back from China
and started waking at 5.

Then I tried to sleep earlier,
and ended up waking at 3.

On Instagram, my swipe reached
a white attic.

Everything in a shade of white,
deliberately,

sophisticatedly
varied, positioned.

Clothing companies
would call this less

white kind of white
"natural."

There is also the term
"off-white,"

which I suppose
is supposed to be

less off-putting.
It all seemed to be

expressing
an extended idea

about effort
and instinct.

Possible shadows
fall into place

before being inhabited
by the real body off-site,

screening
before the screen.

✹

He says everything
is made to move

by a secret, airy density in his head.
The colors are too innocent to be actual.

Then he transforms an aggressive loneliness
into a hypnotic obstinance.

Plump dresses
feed into the billowing of his mind.

Women walk towards houses
with such an attractive sense of entitlement.

Their intentions are distant by now.
They are finally safe to him,

ready to embody
his particular longing.

✳

The specificity of my own body at times
overshadows the specificity of yours.

Sometimes connection becomes
a war of focus.

Someone touches on something,
then a numbness, or a dire receptivity.

Only in English could I
somehow reinstate my consciousness.

Have I loved it the way
we would never know?

Journey to the West

Interview: Monkey

I looked out of the window. There was
a sudden breathability to the air
and I forgot whether I was hungry

or just very tired.
It had been three years
since I had changed into anything.

*

They would rather hear me speak
what they did not understand
so they could just relax, and watch me.

I smiled like a machine
and tried to manage the desirability
of my weirdness and I could,

near the end, tell
that they relaxed
and regarded me as artistic.

When you asked me to appear I hesitated.

I had decided that I would not talk
with those who dare
speak for me.

✴

I always reminded Master
Master straighten your back.
You want to appear stiff
to these monsters, not supple.

You signal how delicious you are
by hunching like this.
The posture of reading is also
a posture of concession.

✳

He asked me
if I would ever consider becoming
a politician here.

He said *I like how much coverage
a U. S. president gets.
All our lives, during*

*the most glorious days, we never
got to appear on TV, and that is
why scholars never got my*

personality right. He was
fascinated by the wide range
of "straight talk."

✳

After a procedure,
during the period of pain
management and delirium,

some say what soothed him
were Donald Trump's
hand movements.

✳

He started in Pure Land Monastery.
There he read Nirvana Sutra.
It presented him a nirvana

much more inclusive,
though diverging interpretations
made him uncertain. He left

for India, in search of source texts.
The court had refused his
application for the permission

to travel. He set out
by joining a caravan,
and we met.

Interview: Pig

On my 290th birthday,
I thought the reason that I had been changed

was that I had not known
how to refuse myself.

Everything seemed like an offer.
Or my mind relentlessly offered

everything.
After all, consumption was a way of
                                    measuring.

✷

      I plowed
      when Master and Monkey
      were meditating.

      I was planting a variety of seeds
      when they were imagining
      the merging of *the three teachings*.

People this obsessed
with comparison

rarely arrive at
a preference.

They grow attached to
the translatability of a choice.

✴

In March and April, I work
as a controlled burns expert.

I make decisions regarding
techniques, timing, and intensities.

Prescribed fires prevent
uncontrolled wildfires.

After each burn, I hand-pull
the invasive species.

✶

In any case like Monkey I do not consider myself
as having a mother,

but I personally do not cultivate
a signature indifference towards

all the women
that cannot be understood.

✳

>I plowed when they were meditating.
>I planted a variety of seeds.

Later, I consumed everything
and gained a completely physical

                                  self-knowledge.

Translator's Note

Translator's Note

There is a morning kindness.
You have to breathe it in.

The sea outside opaque like milk.
They call it austere,

but it's the kind of tenderness
that persists

like a piece of furniture,
supporting even emptiness.

I remember those white animal sculptures
between the beach and the road near my old home—

the 12 animals from the Chinese zodiac.
How I used to climb them all.

One gradually acquires a methodology.
Depending on the shape of the thigh,

the butt, or the tail,
you set your foot

onto the edge of a hollow,
or a curve.

In short,
you make use of the edges—

those hard, solidified contours
of a stylized figure.

You'll start to appreciate simplification,
that smoothness.

✳

In 2009, I read the news about two bronze zodiac
    animal heads
being returned to China.

The heads used to have
anthropomorphic bodies,

which were burned
along with the palace.

Every few years, a head or two
appears at auctions.

✳

You linger longer and wait
for an old boredom
to catch up with you
so you can feel safe.
How much importance
can you trust now?

This familiar pungent smell
of the sea—your identity is in it.
It's more straightforward
than your own body.

Stand across the road
from the sculptures. Why
do they look so cold now?
What is it about beauty
that always makes one aware of the silent
standard raised by loneliness?

✳

Throughout the night,
the sea offers waves and waves of permission.

Translator's Note

Admittedly I had not slept well
and felt passive
like a doorframe
of my self.

Time slows down
all the tiny embodiments of moments

you give
without witness.

You keep on adding memory
to modify the overall

form of your memory
of yourself.

You even recompose yourself to justify
the language you used

extraordinarily
misleadingly.

✳

The living room
in half-light,

I sit here thinking
am I feeling, not thinking.

*am I simply enjoying a rare
separation of feelings?*

I walk across the room
(Am I thinking of him

as geography—
how his face varied

rhythmically, calmly,
objectively.)

Over-understanding
frightens one,

as by over-understanding
one becomes alone again.

Then again,
there was a time we were in awe

of each other's demand.
You made a joke

about isolation
in a restaurant at noon.

The shapes of others
seemed brighter

as they went further.
From a distance,

they were reflective like paper.
Certain roles erased us.

I reminded myself
who I thought I was.

The world settled swiftly
pursuing a better exhaustion.

Translator's Note

Last winter, you watched the members of your family—
that is, the three of you—settle in their own ways
in an emergency room.

You felt a loss in this kind of knowledge about family,
as if you had started to fear that all of you
might lose your ability to comment on each other.

If god exists,
he must be in the ceiling light of
every hospital.

The body was a given thing.
Its clarity is now convincing
beyond control.

My father looked at the floor
silently, up to a point.

My mother and I kept asking
the questions we thought
were worth asking.

Humanity is different
from being human.

Humanity is a faith
in all the unnatural efforts
you made.

Translator's Note

Yet I have served you to the point
of vagueness.

As one translates one's abstractions,
loneliness becomes irrevocable.

Yet how phrases always turn
and redeem themselves

with self-knowledge.
There seems to be

an integrity
without purpose.

✺

The night Lulu drove us back from Chicago,
we passed by a field of wind turbines.

They blinked their red lights rhythmically
calmly, objectively.

Within the unlit durations,
the sky was dilated,

the music in the car
substantial.

The singing voice
pressed down.

So certain sounds were the breathable nature
of certain quiet.

So the precision you always sought
had been yours.

Translator's Note

She presses her paper onto the pane
and makes this physical use of light.

The brightness thins the paper
till a shape is clear.

✳

There is no word for *dying*, the present participle,
in Chinese.

One could say that it starts with being
born.

Zhuangzi would stress that it started with the birth
of all.

Let's call it the point where differentiation
creates a field of attachment.

(You think you are only attached to reason,
but you are attached to how reason attaches

and makes you feel, occasionally, that
there is no need to reason further.)

From being subject to attachment,
one learns that attachment is subject to everything.

✷

The doctor says another's organ might be needed at some point.

You just don't know how to measure the soul alone.

✱

She was forcing a skeleton of shadow to stand up.

Vertical, unlike a real shadow,

the trace did not need to touch the heel of the living shape,

and there was no obligation to always lay the self down.

✱

The speaker stands in the foyer,

the sounds sliding down in the door she has just opened.

✱

This part of life in another country

becomes the animal one may slip into.

✴

That year back in China,
my inside was gleaming
whenever I wrote English.

It was the thrill
of finally admitting the condition
of meaning something alone.

The escapist
is also the obsessed,
insisting on

certain irreplaceability—
the manner of meaning
meaningful on its own,

but sometimes movement
replaces the one
meant to be moved.

Empson writes about
the return of the meaning
to the speaker.

Sometimes that return is
embarrassing
to the self.

Pages shut.
The physical need
is just to have

what has happened
press what is to come
tight again.

Translator's Note

Considering all the units of isolated tenderness,
you know the beauty of Chinese

and the beauty of English
cannot coexist in one language, but coexist.

You walked out of the building
and stood in the sun.

You had a hard time telling him
his form of racism was unquotable.

✳

In the movie, the man follows
the boy slowly.

This stability of movement seems to comfort
both the man and the camera.

They steadily straighten a path
for the boy walking in the middle.

When the man and the boy officially fall
in love, they reach the bottom of a waterfall.

The whole scene dissolves
into the waterfall alone,

the sound of the waterfall much heavier
than its own whiteness.

✳

The park called Forest Park
seemed indeed like a forest

from this angle of the art museum,
the night leaning towards my face.

I started to feel masculinity like a tree—
all that rustling amplitude.

Translator's Note

> —after Li Wenliang (1985-2020)

Without pedestrians, our cities
look like the top half of a feeling.

Translator's Note

Only language fell
into this divided field,

political
to the point of graininess,

apolitical.
Words went weightless

as they started
the descent

within. You still
believe in free

speech, though you
watched language

attack its own body
without end,

like the immune
system of a real

body, infected
by the real

virus.

✺

During
the deadly days,

only the television
talked.

In order to fall
asleep,

I imagined
my best audience

watching me fall
asleep

at the center of a large
bedroom.

The pause in
a voice reached

somewhere else
about us.

To Compare

The air takes gulps
of rain at an angle.

Inside, on hold,
our varieties

of willingness.
Then, the reverb

of the librarian's
answer,

the patience
around circulation,

the small sounds
behind the rows

of computers,
the subtle

Buddhist inhale of
the central air

conditioning
in an institution

of higher education.
Outside, the midday

by now
unrecognizable,

like the monsoon
back home.

To Compare

A. Glenn Gould, *Goldberg Variations* (1956)

The fingers reach a perfect speed:
you cannot distinguish pressing
from summing up.

We inherit these momentums
from our parents, and perhaps
the parents of others

who, despite speaking differently,
mapped out the smoothness
of the rest of the earth.

✹

B. Glenn Gould, *Goldberg Variations* (1982)

"The rest of the earth"
is a territory.
It has convinced
me of the price

of classical
tenderness.
I press on
the shoulders of

"the rest of the earth."
It promises
to yield.
Hum

to things sinking
under my hand.

Land Art

He disappeared behind branches of frost
and distracted the landscape.

How deliberate is a silhouette,
a man alone
      along nature—
how fluent can it be?
He has watched a person
move in a crowd—the human tide easily
alleviated him,
but in a landscape, a person
is a mote of brown complexity,
with banal grief, like twigs,
or banal ecstasy, like twigs.

He did not think
he would be accepted by natural light
so assuringly.

Notes

The Megan Garber epigraph on pg. 19 is taken from her article "Do You Speak Fox?: How Donald Trump's favorite news source became a language," published online in *The Atlantic* on Sept. 16, 2020.

Acknowledgments

Thank you to the editors of the following publications for featuring poems from this collection, sometimes in different versions (including the Chinese version/self-translation): *Bennington Review*, *Gulf Coast*, *Oxford Poetry*, *Poetry*, *Prototype*, *Shikan* (诗刊 Poetry magazine) and the anthology *Wo ting jian le shi jian : jue qi de Zhongguo 90 hou shi ren* (我听见了时间：崛起的中国90后诗人 *I have heard time: the rising of Chinese poets born in the 1990s*).

Thank you to my first readers: Baba Badji, Mary Jo Bang, Kōan Brink, Joshua Cohen, Trevin Corsiglia, Matthias Göritz, Gwyneth Henke, Ignacio Infante, Katy Lederer, Derick Mattern, Sarah María Medina, Steven Meyer, Alex Mouw, Anca Parvulescu, Alice Quinn, Vincent Sherry, Jess Shollenberger, Lynne Tatlock, Yihan Lulu Wang, and everyone associated with the International Writers Track in Comparative Literature at Washington University in St. Louis.

Thank you to my editor, Jeff Alessandrelli. Thank you to the cover and text designer of this book, Mike Corrao. Thank you to everyone at Fonograf Editions.

Thank you to my mother, father, and Trevin.

Thank you to Lucie Brock-Broido (1956–2018) and Saskia Hamilton (1967–2023).

FONOGRAF

1. **Eileen Myles**—*Aloha/irish trees* (LP)
2. **Rae Armantrout**—*Conflation* (LP)
3. **Alice Notley**—*Live in Seattle* (LP)
4. **Harmony Holiday**—*The Black Saint and the Sinnerman* (LP)
5. **Susan Howe & Nathaniel Mackey**—*STRAY: A Graphic Tone* (LP)
6. **Annelyse Gelman & Jason Grier**—*About Repulsion* (EP)
7. **Joshua Beckman**—*Some Mechanical Poems To Be Read Aloud* (print)
8. **Dao Strom**—*Instrument/ Traveler's Ode* (print; cassette tape)
9. **Douglas Kearney & Val Jeanty**—*Fodder* (LP)
10. **Mark Leidner**—*Returning the Sword to the Stone* (print)
11. **Charles Valle**—*Proof of Stake: An Elegy* (print)
12. **Emily Kendal Frey**—*LOVABILITY* (print)
13. **Brian Laidlaw and the Family Trade**—*THIS ASTER: adaptations of Emile Nelligan* (LP)
14. **Nathaniel Mackey and The Creaking Breeze Ensemble**—*Fugitive Equation* (compact disc)
15. *FE Magazine* (print)
16. **Brandi Katherine Herrera**—*MOTHER IS A BODY* (print)
17. **Jan Verberkmoes**—*Firewatch* (print)
18. **Krystal Languell**—*Systems Thinking with Flowers* (print)
19. **Matvei Yankelevich**—*Dead Winter* (print)
20. **Cody-Rose Clevidence**—*Dearth & God's Green Mirth* (print)
21. **Hilary Plum**—*Hole Studies* (print)
22. **John Ashbery**—*Live at Sanders Theatre, 1976* (LP)

23. **Alice Notley**—*The Speak Angel Series* (print)

24. **Alice Notley**—*Early Works* (print)

25. **Joshua Marie Wilkinson**—*Trouble Finds You* (print)

26. **Timmy Straw**—*The Thomas Salto* (print)

27. **Audre Lorde**—*At Fassett Studio, 1970* (LP)

28. **Gabriel Palacios**—*A Ten Peso Burial For Which Truth I Sign* (print)

29. **Isabel Zapata, trans. Robin Myers**—*A Whale Is a Country* (print)

30. **Callum Angus**—*Cataract* (print)

31. **Eds. Dao Strom & Jyothi Natarajan**—*A Mouth Holds Many Things: A De-Canon Hybrid-Literary Collection* (print)

32. **Cody-Rose Clevidence**—*The Grimace of Eden, Now* (print)

33. **Jaydra Johnson**—*Low: Notes on Art and Trash* (print)

34. **Jaime Gil de Biedma**—*If Only For a Moment (I'll Never Be Young Again)* (print)

35. **Esther Kondo Heller**—*AR:RANGE:MENTS* (print)

36. **Ahmad Almallah**—*Wrong Winds* (print)

37. **Kimberly Alidio**—*Traceable Relation* (print)

38. **Sara Gilmore**—*The Green Lives* (print)

39. **Darcie Dennigan**—*Little Neck* (print)

40. **Nora Claire Miller**—*Groceries* (print)

41. **Rachel Rahmé**—*Mercurial, or is that Liberty?* (print)

42. **Eileen Myles**—*Bird Watching and Their First Three Books of Poetry* (print)

43. **Kristen Gleason**—*The Wallet and Other Thefts* (print)

Fonograf Editions is a registered 501(c)(3) nonprofit organization. Find more information about the press at: fonografeditions.com.